The Agile Change Playbook

Dr Jen Frahm & Lena Ross

A catalogue record for this work is available from the National Library of Australia

ACN 633 844 103

Frahm, Dr Jen *(Author)* Ross, Lena *(Author)*
The Agile Change Playbook
ISBN: 978-1-922452-79-5

Cover design: Amelia Lazarus
Published by Green Hill Publishing

AUTHORS' NOTE

We've written this during the very strange time that was COVID19 #stayathome. We had the idea of a book on the product roadmap and when our workshops ceased suddenly, it seemed a good idea to prioritise!

In writing during this time, the context has highlighted the need for remote tools and practices. The handy thing is that many agile teams have been working remotely for decades, so while your initial preference might be getting people in a room and working with a whiteboard, or flipchart - you will find there are dozens of software tools and platforms designed to facilitate all of these practices remotely. By all means, drop us a line if you are struggling with how, but our suggestion would be to catch up with an agile coach in your company, tell them what you want to do and ask how they would do it with one of the teams in another country.

You may find language in this Playbook that is different to what you are used to. The hallmarks of an Agile Change Adventurer are curiosity and resourcefulness. Perhaps keep a notepad by your side to capture words or terms you don't understand so you can google and investigate further.

We practise what we preach – we co-created the Agile Change Leadership Institute by working out loud in increments and learning from our failures. Everything in this Playbook book has been tested and applied in real organisations with real stakeholders.

ACKNOWLEDGEMENTS

As always, the writing and production of a new book occurs within the support of a community. We are both very grateful to our family, friends, clients, our business community, our friends from the Change Community Hub, and our friends from the Change Management Institute along with our special reviewers - Joanne King and Paul Winbanks.

DEDICATION

This book is dedicated to all of the brave Agile Change Adventurers out there prepared to give things a go, experiment, learn out loud and play with new ideas!

TABLE OF CONTENTS

WARNING

This Playbook is likely to **change** the
way you deliver change!

INTRODUCTION

Why we wrote this Playbook

Welcome to the Agile Change Playbook - if you've come this far it's probably because you have landed in the wild world of agile projects and initiatives, or an organization that is 'going agile'. Your existing toolkit is a good one, but it doesn't quite fit the new world. That was our experience about seven years ago when we both started dipping our collective toes in the world of agile. Over the years we have experimented, played, failed, and adapted in various fashions with our change practice. We've pulled that experience together in this Playbook.

Build a common understanding of Big A and little a

If you're working in an organization that's had little or no exposure to agile, you may find yourself in a situation where you may need to explain the difference between big A and little a agile?'

The two versions of the word agile - capitalised and all lower case - are often used interchangeably.

Big A refers to the agile approach derived from software development. Small a refers to the pursuit of business agility.

This Playbook mainly looks at how to do change using Agile tools and techniques but is not limited to project change. The practices we share can also be used in broader transformation efforts to be more agile as a business.

How to use it?

Oh, on that, why is it a playbook and not a handbook? It's intentional. Not all of the agile change tools in this playbook will work for you; you're going to have to play with them and work out which ones suit, and which ones you might use on another initiative. You don't have to work through this sequentially; that's the thing with agile change - while we need to place pages in order to produce this book, it's unlikely you will use them in that order!

Don't wait until you're told to go 'agile'!

The agile change practices we cover in this Playbook can be applied regardless of the 'change methodology' or 'framework' you have in place in your organization. Whether or not your project is officially declared to be an agile one, there's no reason why you can't introduce these agile change practices in your work as a change leader or manager.

The idea is to try them out. It's about introducing change activity that is lighter and 'right-sized' for your change initiative and business. The intent is to invite and nudge people to contribute and iterate. You'll be surprised at how your colleagues will notice the incremental changes and how liberating your practice will become.

Our practice is evolving

The focus is on emergent practice rather than what we have been taught as best practice. You might call it next practice. With every change comes opportunity, and as change is constant, you will continually learn. We need to deliver change differently and engage our people in the spirit of co-creation and collaboration. It's exciting times for change practitioners, as your role will continue to evolve!

Drop your tools

There's a sobering case study of how a small group of fire-fighters survived a catastrophic fire in Mann Gulch, USA in 1949. The majority of experienced firefighters held onto their tools and tried to run to safe spaces. The weight of their tools prevented them from getting to safety. Thirteen died. Three survived. The ones who survived did so because they recognised the changing conditions and dropped their tools. This was incredibly difficult to do and speaks to identity change and ingrained habits. Like wildfire, agile is taking over our workplaces. If change practitioners wish to survive, they need to drop their tools. And pick up new ones.

Safety first!

When you experiment, let your stakeholders know you are testing a practice or activity, so you can manage the expectation that it may not be perfect, and it may need iteration.

When your intent is right, and you broadcast that you are experimenting with an idea, you create a safe place to test and learn.

Now, let's explore ways to do it!

IDEAS:

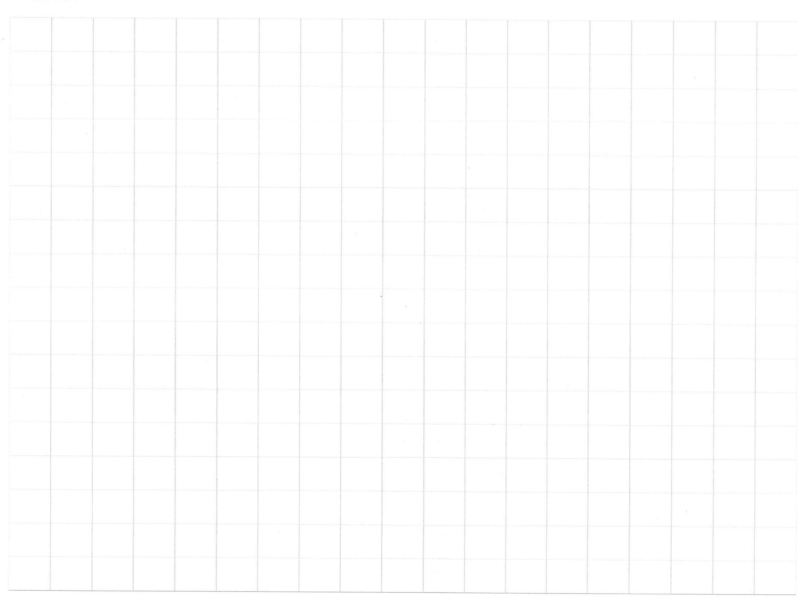

Part One

HOW DID WE GET HERE?

Agile is not just for techies!
Agile is **everybody's** business!

MAKING SENSE OF AGILE

Where we came from

For a long time where linear, waterfall-style projects were mainstream, change was delivered in a step-by-step approach with a list of artefacts to complete. Now, in a climate of complex and continuous change, there is an increasing expectation that change programs will be leaner and deliver outcomes in shorter cycles. This means change practitioners will encounter agile as a way of *doing* and *being* in their work.

Entire books, in the thousands, have been written about agile with various perspectives. For the change practitioner to understand what it means, it's best to start by exploring agile in the context of the Agile Manifesto.

Here we are

It's now likely that we'll find ourselves in workplaces that are transforming to new or agile ways of working. In our adaptation, there is a compelling need to demonstrate agility in our mindset, behaviours and practice. It's time to make sense of what this really means, not just for leaders, but for all employees, so we can play a meaningful role to support and continue to create the future of work.

What this means for us

Change practitioners can apply agile practices to any change initiative - it doesn't have to be a project that is officially labelled as an 'agile' one. Agile practices are people-centric ones that promote deep engagement. There is no 'one-way, same way' to do 'agile change'. Think of it as a smorgasbord of practices that you pick from to suit the organization and the change initiative you're working on. It draws on a range of agile and lean practices and needs an agile mindset and approach to adapt it so it's right for your environment.

> Agile is a way of thinking, a set of behaviours as well as being a set of practices.
> *Lena Ross*

It's about **being** agile and **doing** agile.

Part Two

THE AGILE MANIFESTO

THE AGILE MANIFESTO

The history of the Big A

To provide some clarity on Agile (yes, with a big A), let's take a brief look at where it started. If you've been reading or talking about Agile/agile, no doubt you've heard of the Agile Manifesto.

The Agile Manifesto, designed for software development, was co-written back in 2001. Its intent was not to be anti-methodology, but to bring about a balanced view that would welcome adjustments and pace. In the Manifesto we can see the elements that are core to change practitioners in an agile world: a focus on the customer, a nimble approach and value placed on people over process.

> While there is value in the items on the right, we value the items on the left more.

The Agile Manifesto is made up of

4 values
12 principles

Over time the values and principles have snowballed to areas that were not software-centric, especially with the themes of lean, team behaviours and customer-centricity.

👥👥 Individuals & interactions	Processes & tools
🔧 Working software	Comprehensive documentation
👥 Customer collaboration	Contract negotiation
↻ Responding to change	Following a plan

SOURCE: www.agilemanifesto.org

THE AGILE MANIFESTO 12 PRINCIPLES

1. Our highest priority is to satisfy the customer through early and continuous delivery of valuable software.

2. Welcome changing requirements, even late in development. Agile processes harness change for the customer's competitive advantage.

3. Deliver working software frequently, from a couple of weeks to a couple of months, with a preference to the shorter timescale.

4. Business people and developers must work together daily throughout the project.

5. Build projects around motivated individuals. Give them the environment and support they need and trust them to get the job done.

6. The most efficient and effective method of conveying information to and within a development team is face-to-face conversation.

7. Working software is the primary measure of progress.

8. Agile processes promote sustainable development. The sponsors, developers, and users should be able to maintain a constant pace indefinitely.

9. Continuous attention to technical excellence and good design enhances agility.

10. Simplicity - the art of maximizing the amount of work not done - is essential.

11. The best architectures, requirements, and designs emerge from self-organizing teams.

12. At regular intervals, the team reflects on how to become more effective, then tunes and adjusts its behaviour accordingly.

Source: www.agilemanifesto.org

ACTION

Over to you
The 12 Agile Principles can be really useful in getting your change team (or yourself if a solo practitioner) focused on what needs to happen.

Take some time out with your team or yourself and a cup of tea and think through how you might adapt the 12 Agile Principles so that they are 12 Agile Change Principles.

You have a template on the next page to do this.

Once complete, print this on an A3 sheet and put it up on a wall nearby or print on A5 size and laminate and keep it with you. You might even post it on your virtual platforms.

This will be helpful when things get really difficult - you can return to first principles and work out what might be the best way forth for agile change.

THE AGILE MANIFESTO MY 12 PRINCIPLES

1. Our highest priority is to ....

2. We welcome change because...

3. Deliver .... from ....to ...., with a preference to the shorter timescale.

4. Business people and ....must work togwether daily to ....

5. Build teams of motivated individuals. Give them .... and ...., and trust them to get the job done.

6. The most efficient and effective method of conveying information to and within a .... team is ....

7. ....is the primary measure of progress.

8. Agile change processes promote sustainable ....   The change sponsor should ....

9. Continuous attention to ....and ....enhances agility.

10. Simplicity - the art of maximizing the amount of work not done is essential. We do this by........................

11. The best ....emerge from self-organizing teams.

12. At regular intervals, the team reflects on how to become more effective, then tunes and adjusts its behaviour accordingly.

NOTES:

NOTES:

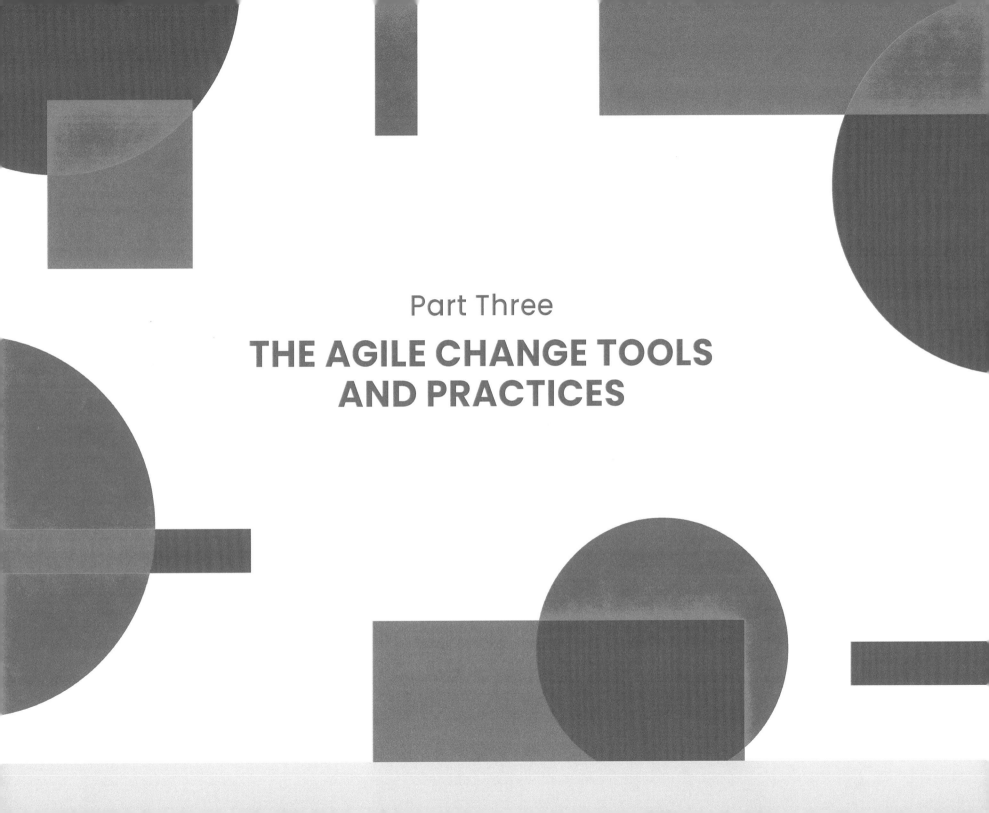

Part Three

THE AGILE CHANGE TOOLS AND PRACTICES

A CAPABILITY APPROACH TO AGILE CHANGE

Why take a capability approach?

Yes, we understand. You don't have the bandwidth or headspace to take in any more change models, processes or frameworks. You're not alone.

This is also the situation for many of your stakeholders. As work speeds up, our capacity to take in new information reduces.

That's why many of the companies that have embraced agile successfully talk to the power of principles. Working with principles instead of a prescribed formula is an approach that's aligned to new and agile ways of working. Principles speed up delivery and provide flexibility.

In an increasingly complex and ambiguous world, we need to draw on a range of tools and techniques so our work and change efforts are fit for purpose, while also promoting sense-making and co-creation.

More benefits

Working with principles instead of a prescribed formula is an approach that's aligned to new and agile ways of working. When we shift to a more iterative approach that responds to what is needed in the moment, we open more possibilities. It helps us approach change plans with a beginner's mindset, rather than assuming all change is planned and delivered in the same way.

It's a mindset shift

Embracing a beginner's mindset can be quite the shift for many people as it means a departure from step-by-step methodologies and processes.

We see the fundamental truths of agile change as consisting of three capabilities. And once you have built those capabilities, you can plug and play the agile tools into any change model or framework.

Letting go

This shift represents a move away from following a change methodology that prescribes a list of artefacts to produce, towards change deliverables that are needed for each specific change and being open to iteration as we progress.

> Boil things down to fundamental truths...and then reason up from there.
> *Elon Musk*

AT THE HEART OF AGILE CHANGE ARE 3 CAPABILITIES:

Data Informed Decision Making

Continuous Engagement

Visual and Transparent Communication

AND 4 CORE PRACTICES:

- Working Out Loud
- Change Data Analysis
- Visual Management
- The Kanban Board

While we have **30 agile change practices** for you to try, if you do nothing else but shift your practice towards these four things, you will fare much better in agile initiatives!

Let's look at these first!

3 AGILE CHANGE CAPABILITIES AND 4 CORE AGILE PRACTICES

ENGAGEMENT

Social Architecture & 3% Rule
Change Ready Check
Lean Coffee
Co-Creation

Reverse Go-Live
60% Done & Shared
Think/Act/Feel
Persona Mapping

Transparent Work
Platforms
Enterprise Social
Networks
Digital Workflow
Collaborative
Documents
Stand-Ups
Change Canvas

FOUR CORE PRACTICES
WORKING OUT LOUD
CHANGE DATA
VISUAL MANAGEMENT
KANBAN BOARDS

Future Changescape
Change Blast Radius
Minimum Viable
(Change) Process
Change Backlog with
T-Shirt Sizing, User Stories &
Story Points
Change Radar

Storytelling
Pecha Kucha
Infographics
Roadmaps
Plan-to-a-Page
Lean Filmmaking

DATA INFORMED DECISION MAKING

Change Scorecard
I like, I wish, What if...
Retrospectives

COMMUNICATION

WORKING OUT LOUD

Tell me about it

Working Out Loud (WOL) is the practice of working publicly and collaboratively to amplify connections, networks, innovation and understanding.

Working Out Loud is the term originally coined by Bryce Williams in 2010 for a practice that radically changes how we perform our work.

It was later advanced by Simon Terry and John Stepper, with Stepper doing a TEDx talk, publishing a book and creating the infrastructure for a global movement and a focused use of the approach with Work Out Loud Circles.

For us, Working Out Loud is a foundation agile change practice and can be applied to all capabilities: data informed decision making, engagement, and communication.

How do you use it?

As Terry suggests, when we 'Work Out Loud' we do so first to connect, then share, then solve problems publicly, which can lead to innovations.

At its most basic, we do this by narrating our work on public platforms – posters by our desk, Yammer, Twitter, or SharePoint – 'I'm working on product x– we're doing [activity]'.

You may see your Agile teams setting up showcases - these are a form of Working Out Loud.

This increases opportunity for connection, then sharing, then collaborative problem solving.

Good to know

If you have a culture that rewards perfection, this will be a high-risk activity.

For this to work you need a genuine invitation to make your work better and a preparedness to receive feedback on your work.

You can feel very vulnerable in sharing work that is not complete. You may want to send your senior leaders material on the benefits of working out loud first.

You can also consider how to introduce WOL as it is a change to the organization.

Hints and tips
- Make your work visible
- Make your work better
- Lead with generosity
- Build a social network
- Make it all purposeful

Working out loud =
observable work +
narrating your work
Bryce Williams

 People over process

 Working software

 Customer collaboration

Jen is working out loud
so please drop in:
MON 1-4pm
WED 9am-12pm

APPLYING IT

- Think about how you will make your work visible – is it online, a wall, a room, a poster?
- Work out what is your request of those who will contribute
- What are you prepared to risk?
- Show people how what you are demonstrating adds value to them
- Note the new connections you are making and consider how you can help them
- Make sure you have a goal attached to your initiative

USE OF CHANGE DATA

Tell me about it

Decision making speeds up in agile initiatives and this is largely enabled by a greater data capability and it's for this reason we have the use of change data placed as a core agile change practice.

Whereas once business analysis was the domain of the Business Analyst (BA), now the user-friendly cloud-based systems mean greater transparency for change practitioners as well.

And while technology makes our life easier, don't forget old fashioned checking in!

How do you use it?

This depends on what you want to measure.

Network influencers (potential change champions). Identify your change champions and influencers through Organizational Network Analysis (ONA) tools such as Swoop Analytics for Yammer.

Change saturation. Measure with tools such as heat maps. Some are automated with Power BI, some are SaaS based, and some are created manually.

Communication effectiveness. Measure with real-time open rates and click throughs with platforms such as Campaign Monitor, Mail Chimp and Adobe eDM.

Feedback on change progress. Measure with pulse checks such as micro survey platforms like Culture Amp or physical attendance at Stand-ups.

Good to know

Your change management data will:
- Inform decision making
- Support and drive conversations with stakeholders
- Help you identify your change success measures
- Guide your change activity

When identifying and documenting your change measures for data, make sure they directly relate to your planned change initiatives and not the overall project implementation deliverables.

Remember, the change practitioner is not responsible for delivering the business benefits of the program of work or the project.

Hints and tips
- Don't overlook what's in front of you – e.g. attendance at stand-ups, lean coffees. These are opportunities to gather data about the change to occur.
- The digital tools you use are rich in real-time data, e.g. social media analytics.
- You can gather quick data through beta testing – to test or prototype a solution or idea.
- Build a great visual change dashboard from your data!

 Responding to change

APPLYING IT

HERE'S AN EXAMPLE FROM A WORKDAY IMPLEMENTATION

WORKDAY GO LIVE CHECKLIST

- ✔ Receive your access email
- ☐ Check and update personal profile, including emergency contacts via the personal information worklet
- ☐ Enter your Let's Talk Goals via the Performance worklet (not applicable for contactors)
- ☐ Update Career Interests via the Career worklet
- ☐ Import Job History from LinkedIn via My Profle > Overview tab
- ☐ Update Job Interests via the Career worklet > Car
- ☐ Enter Relocation Preference via the Career workle
- ☐ Enter Travel Preferences via the Career worklet >

Then we looked at the WORLD VIEW to see where emails were opened.

OPENS	CLICKS	SHARES
13,628	3,324	0

VISUAL MANAGEMENT

Tell me about it

Visual Management (VM) is a way of working transparently so people can get as much information in as little amount of time.

While many Working Out Loud practices involve working transparently, they are usually done for the purpose of engagement and co-creation.

Visual Management is more about communicating complex information as simply as possible and tracking progress and you will see it used it many agile change practices.

How do you use it?

Visual Management is a practice derived from the Lean movement.

Lean seeks to eradicate waste in the system, thus simplifying and speeding the system up, and originates from Toyota in the 1980s.

It complements the Agile principle of simplicity – the art of maximising the amount of work NOT done.

Good to know

Our brains process visual information faster by processing multiple images at the one time.

As attention spans become shorter, we need to be clever about how we communicate and capture information.

FUN FACT!
Did you know that the human brain processes visual information 60,000 times faster than text?

Hints and tips

- Engage someone on your team skilled at communication to set this up – VM is not printing out a spreadsheet on an A3 sheet of paper!
- Run your team stand-ups and stakeholder meetings at your VM board.
- Refresh it with new information regularly to maintain interest.
- Use VM to show the progress of your change work along with other relevant aspects of your change initiative.

 People over process

 Working software

 Customer collaboration

 Responding to change

APPLYING IT

USE YOUR ICONS

CHANGE SATURATION

CHANGE READINESS

WHO'S ON THE TEAM

Team structure

Chapter

Squad

Sprint Review team

Product Owner

KANBAN BOARD

Tell me about it

Kanban is the Japanese word for 'visual signal' or 'visual card'.

Inspired by the Lean manufacturing practices at Toyota, the Kanban board is an effective way for teams to visually display what they are working on and where it's at and identify blockers or impediments to progress. You will find it extremely useful and a foundation of many agile change practices.

How do you use it?

Make your Kanban highly visible on your Visual Management board.

Consider online Kanban boards for your remote and distributed teams.

Use post-it notes or small cards.

Good to know

One of the objectives of the Kanban board is to bring attention to the volume of work in progress – in the DOING column – to reduce it.

The idea is to move the work along the flow, to the DONE column.

At a glance, you not only see the progress of the work, but also the scope and scale of the work underway.

The Kanban board is likely to attract attention from people walking by, making it an effective tool to create interest and kick off conversations about your change initiative.

Hints and tips
- Run stand-up and stakeholder meetings at your Kanban board.
- Add avatars to each card to show ownership and make it even more visual.

 People over process

 Working software

 Customer collaboration

 Responding to change

APPLYING IT

THE KANBAN BOARD

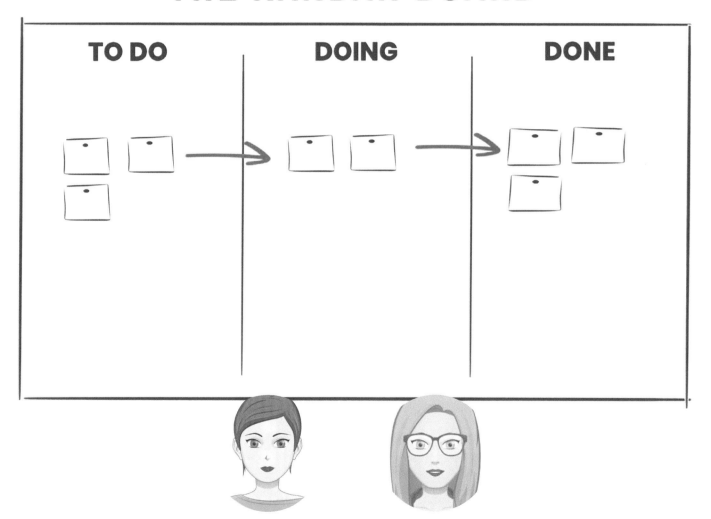

YOU'VE SEEN FOUR CORE AGILE CHANGE PRACTICES

Want more? Great!
Read on...

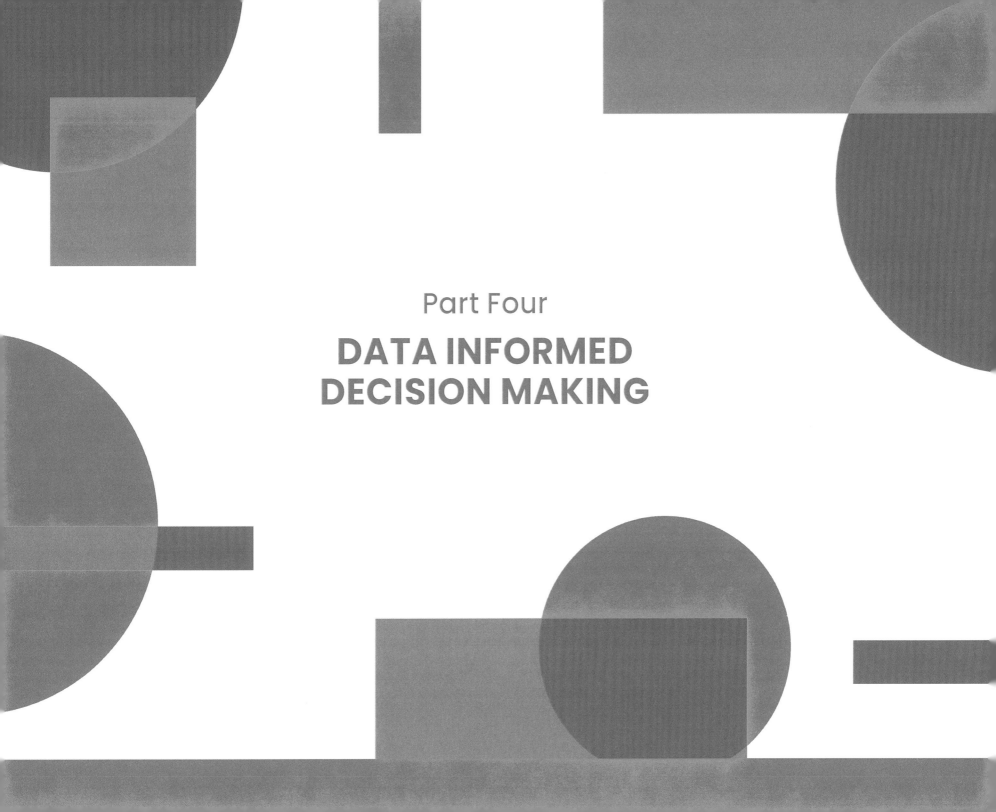

Part Four

DATA INFORMED
DECISION MAKING

DATA INFORMED DECISION MAKING

It's one of those universal truisms in change. The more work you put in upfront, the better the result when you launch your change. This is the same for the core capability of analysis which informs data informed decision making – and the reason why this section is the largest and the very first!

> Without data, you are just another person with an opinion.
> *W. Edwards Deming*

WHAT WORK DO WE HAVE TO DO?
Minimum Viable Change Process (MVCP)
Change Backlog
T-Shirt Sizing
Story Points
Change Blast Radius
Change Radar

WHAT ARE THE CHANGE IMPACTS?
Think/Act/Feel
I like, I wish, What if?

WHO ARE OUR STAKEHOLDERS?
Personas

HOW WILL WE CONTINUALLY IMPROVE?
Retrospectives
Futurespective/
Future Changescape

HOW WILL WE ANTICIPATE AND TRACK PROGRESS?
Change Scorecard

Look out for these icons to see which ones apply to each agile practice!

 People over process

 Working software

 Customer collaboration

 Responding to change

MINIMUM VIABLE CHANGE PROCESS (MVCP)

Tell me about it

The Minimum Viable [Change] Process (MVCP) is a take on Agile's Minimum Viable Product (MVP) where you define what is the smallest (and least effort) product you can release that will meet a customer's need.

In a world where large change teams are rare, and change resourcing has become quite lean, it is necessary to establish the minimum change management work you can do and still remain effective.

How do you use it?

Having a MVCP workshop or discussion is essential in managing senior stakeholder expectations. For instance, initiate a discussion on carving out boundaries of what you won't be doing and also ensuring support for what you need to do. In the same way a MVP is defined in collaboration with customers, your MVCP is defined in collaboration with the business stakeholders.

Good to know

Your business stakeholders are often invested in 'OKRs'. OKR stands for Objectives and Key Results and are a popular way to managing performance and progress in Agile environments. Learning to have conversations from your senior stakeholders' perspective, e.g. Knowing their OKRs (goals and desired outcomes) helps you prioritise what is in your MVCP or defend the elimination of change activities.

Your ability to determine the MVCP is enhanced if:

- You are clear on what the business benefits are to be achieved.
- You are clear about the capability of your resources. For example, are they:
  - Multi-skilled?
  - Early career?
  - Mid career?
  - Later career?
- You know the financial modelling of the project and what the Return On Investment (ROI) of your MVCP will be.

Hints and tips

- Make this a collaborative conversation, you don't have to work it out by yourself.
- Be open to other people in the business wanting experience in change and give them tasks to stretch themselves.
- Challenge your mindset – move from 'we can't do this' to 'how could we do this?'

 Working software

 Customer collaboration

MAP OUT WHAT YOU WANT TO ACHIEVE

1. Identify what you need to achieve – i.e. in bullet points.

2. Draw phases of the change and time markers.

3. Use post-it notes to record what you need to do to achieve the change focus – i.e. awareness, consumption, proficiency.

PHASE 3
ONE YEAR ON

PROFICIENCY

PHASE 2
APR–SEP

CONSUMPTION

PHASE 1
JAN–MAR

AWARENESS

- Employees are aware
- Managers can use Workday with assistance from Self Service or People
- Managers know about talent pools function and find worker
- Managers have verified their employees skills and experience
- People team can assist in knowledge transfer and how to use Workday

- Employees submit leave and request feedback for Performance Conversations, and use Workday for pay slips
- Managers can use Workday Independently
- Managers have moved their personal networks to a personal talent pool
- People Team can do compensation and succession planning using Workday

- Employees use Workday as a Business as Usual tool
- Managers are conducting a global find worker seach as routine activity and looking beyond personal networks
- People Team can proactively approach business stakeholders with insights and reports on their business and strategies

APPLYING IT

THEN ...

Map out on paper what you would be doing if you had no boundaries and all the resources in the world.

- Mark those activities that have a direct correlation to benefits realisation.
- Identify those activities that are nice to have and those that are necessary.
- Identify those activities that take long periods of time to do – ask yourself, if we only had a day, what would we do to get the same outcome?

This becomes your MCVP.

CHANGE BACKLOG

Tell me about it

A backlog in the Agile world is the single source of truth of what needs to be worked on, how much effort it will take and what its priority is. You don't work on anything unless it is on the backlog.

Each backlog item has a description – often presented as a user story *(see page 31)*, or what's known as the 'definition of done'. This provides guidance to team members on what they have to do on each item, and they can do it autonomously.

We can take this concept and create a Change Backlog. This is often done after defining the MVCP.

How do you use it?

The change team takes the MVCP or the Reverse Go-Live *(see page 55)* and breaks that down to individual tasks.

You may wish to do this with post-it notes and a physical wall, or you may wish to use a virtual solution, e.g. Jira, Trello.

Good to know

The backlog is dynamic - you can remove backlog items if things change as you realise that the item will not contribute to a valuable change outcome.

Adding to the backlog is only done with agreement of the backlog owner (Change Lead / Product Owner).

Backlog grooming is a best practice to make sure your list of 'things to do' does not become unwieldy or irrelevant.

Remember, in change projects in agile organizations, things change quickly! It's helpful to have sessions on a semi-regular basis to review the backlog and tidy it up.

Hints and tips

- Create your backlog collaboratively – this is best done as a team. The first time you do one, consider asking your Scrum Master or Agile Coach for help as this is a regular practice for them.
- Give ownership of workload to your team.
- Use your backlog as a conversation facilitator with your sponsor – they can see what still has to be done.

 Working software

 Customer collaboration

APPLYING IT

WHAT'S IN THE CHANGE BACKLOG?

User Stories

As a collaboration tool, User Stories are created from the user's perspective.

You can use them to bring the internal customer, or your change recipient to life and replaces the old stakeholder identification and engagement matrices.

Gather them in workshops and invite users to post them on your Visual Management board.

Keep them simple and short – on post-it notes or on index cards.

Make sure you do it from the perspective of the change process – not the software, process, or project deliverable.

T-Shirt Sizing

T-Shirt Sizing is a way that Agile teams work out how much work effort and budget is needed, e.g. small, medium and large.

It's a creative form of relative estimation and gives team members a novel way to talk about what has to be done and how much effort.

Story Points

Another way of estimating relative effort on your change backlog is to give each activity a story point, e.g. 5, 10, 50 and 100. So relative to effort, your sprint might look like:

- Review conversations on Yammer – 5 points.
- Email update to the business – 10 points.
- High level change impact analysis for the call centre team - 50 points.
- When you can work out how many points you can complete as a team for each sprint, you can then identify user stories as weighted points.

USER STORY

As a... General Manager

I need... to be assured of the change impacts

So that I can... plan for business continuity

Change Team Member: LH

USER STORY

As a... Call Centre Operator

I need... to be trained in the new system

So that I can... feel confident and capable

Change Team Member: SK

CHANGE BLAST RADIUS

Tell me about it

A Change Blast Radius is a lean change technique for mapping the stakeholders visually by the following characteristics:

- Degree of impact
- Degree of influence
- Degree of flexibility
- Degree of difficulty in changing

How do you use it?

Traditionally, we would do large stakeholder and change impact analysis activities where we establish power versus influence, such as Mendelow's grid, and size of impact across process, behaviour and technology. These would all be separate documents.

Now, we set up a chart / page or wall with concentric circles and a key to understand the characteristics.

Good to know

This is a high-level analysis and can change from sprint to sprint. Do not over invest time or effort in creating it.

The overall objective is to create an 'easy to digest' visual view of your data for decisions and conversations.

Hints and tips

- Do this activity collaboratively. You will need representatives of the teams impacted and product owners who know the degree of impact.

 People over process

 Customer collaboration

APPLYING IT

CHANGE INITIATIVE
A new software platform for taking calls and recording complaints.

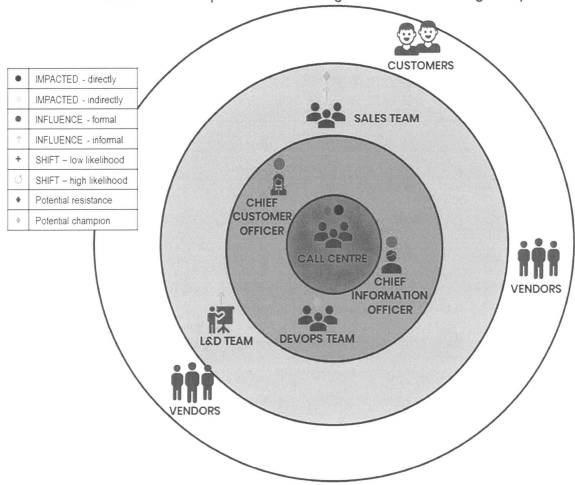

●	IMPACTED - directly
○	IMPACTED - indirectly
●	INFLUENCE - formal
↑	INFLUENCE - informal
✦	SHIFT – low likelihood
↻	SHIFT – high likelihood
◆	Potential resistance
◇	Potential champion

CUSTOMERS

SALES TEAM

CHIEF CUSTOMER OFFICER

CALL CENTRE

CHIEF INFORMATION OFFICER

VENDORS

L&D TEAM

DEVOPS TEAM

VENDORS

CHANGE RADAR

Tell me about it

A Change Radar is an important tool to facilitate conversations with senior stakeholders on how much change is happening and change capacity.

The analogy for capacity we use is an airport runway.

We know that most runways can only ever land one or two big planes within a fixed time, with capacity of a few smaller planes also allowed to land.

If you try to land too many big planes at the same time, things will go badly wrong.

How do you use it?

In your initial stage of scoping and analysis:

1. Ask questions about what other changes are occurring in the next six months (or the time frame that your change needs to happen in).
2. Work out what the relative sizing is of those other changes.
3. Then map those changes onto a radar view.

Good to know

As an analytical tool, the Change Radar helps you answer the question:

Are we landing too much change?

Or what other change might we also deliver at the same time?

It is a tool for generating conversations and more engaging than dashboard reporting.

Hints and tips

- Make the horizontal lines in your radar represent time horizons.
- Your vertical 'wedges' might represent business units.
- Use colour to 'code' your initiatives.
- Shape your balls or icons in size according to the scale of the change.

 People over process

 Customer collaboration

APPLYING IT

CHANGE RADAR

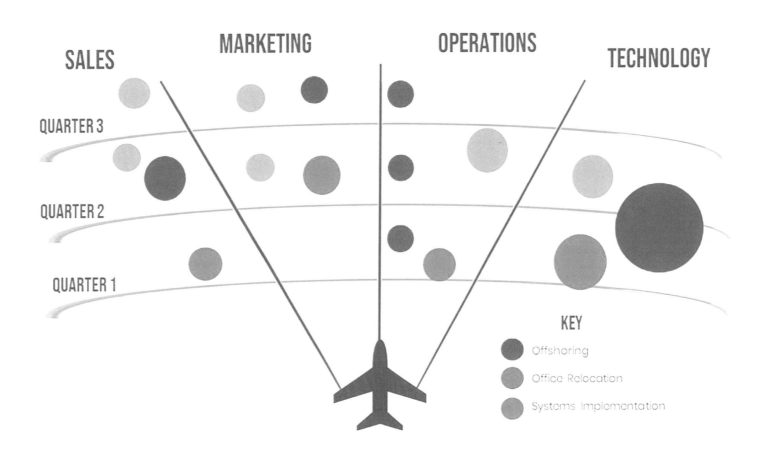

THINK, ACT, FEEL

Tell me about it

Think / Act / Feel is a valuable framework in understanding what is the current state and future state of your change recipients in relation to the change to be delivered. It borrows from the practices of user experience (UX) and design thinking toolkits to understand the change recipient journey. In this way, it can replace the traditional stakeholder identification activities and the traditional change impact analysis.

It offers three benefits:

1. Develops a more empathic view of the change recipient.
2. Identifies pain points to be supported or solved.
3. Identifies opportunities to be amplified.

How do you use it?

Identify what your change recipients are currently thinking, doing and feeling. Then consider what might be the appropriate transitions over the course of the change you are introducing.

This allows you to plan what type of support they will need and manage the metrics of change.

Good to know

Traditional change management has a strong focus on what people are doing, or the processes involved.

Use the template provided to uncover the Think/Act/Feel insights. This is an ideal starting point to understanding your business AND the people in it.

A process map captures actions – the DOING.

Running this activity provides a safe forum for end users to explore rather than just the DOING – they can openly discuss how they are FEELING and what they are THINKING.

This enables us to move to a deeper level of engagement – from engagement to empathy.

Hints and tips

- Prepare the following template as a flip chart and have post-it notes handy.
- Make sure the people filling out the post-it notes are representative of the real users / employees / customers.

 People over process

 Customer collaboration

APPLYING IT

THINK...ACT...FEEL

	PHASE 1	PHASE 2	PHASE 3

WHAT ARE THEY DOING?

What will your impacted users be DOING in the current and/or future state?
For the future state, ask your users:
Imagine yourself in the future state – What are you **doing**? How do you explain it to others?

WHAT ARE THEY THINKING?

For the future state, ask your users:
Imagine yourself in this future state – What are your **thoughts** about what you are doing, the process, the experience?

WHAT ARE THEY FEELING?

For the future state, ask:
Visualise yourself in this future state – How are you **feeling** about what you are doing, the process, the experience? Is it a positive or negative emotion?
How does it make you feel?

EXPERIENCE

Use this row if impacted users currently, or plan to interact with other people, e.g. other teams or business units.
Ask: What is the interaction experience like? Collaborative? Challenging?
What are the current PAIN POINTS? Any expected PAIN POINTS in the future?

WHAT COULD CHANGE?

Consider what has been recorded in the DOING, THINKING and FEELING rows.
What are the OPPORTUNITIES to improve the user experience?

REMEMBER

We said how useful the Kanban format is?

The next three agile change tools rely on a Kanban Board format to demonstrate the data and analysis!

I LIKE...I WISH...WHAT IF?

I LIKE HOW WE... (something that already exists)

I WISH WE COULD... (something I'd like to see in the future state)

WHAT IF/I WONDER IF we tried this what might happen?

RETROSPECTIVE

WHAT WENT WELL?

WHAT WENT LESS WELL?

NEXT TIME WE WILL...

FUTURE CHANGESCAPE

IMAGINE WE HAVE LANDED THE CHANGE

WHAT DOES GOOD LOOK LIKE?

WHAT HELPED US GET THERE?

WHAT GO IN THE WAY?

I LIKE, I WISH, WHAT IF?

Tell me about it

This is a structured format for feedback on changes that is derived from the d.school (the home of design thinking).

The use of the word 'I' in front of the sentence encourages open communication and reduces defensive responses.

With this framing you invite positive and constructive feedback.

How do you use it?

You can use it in groups, or pairs.

Take your change Plan-on-a-Page to your stakeholder and ask them to respond on a template that has the 'I like, I wish, what if' headings.

Or take the initial solution design of the change you are planning to introduce and use this format to gather feedback.

In this way it becomes a tool for co-creation.

Good to know

You can even use this format as a team retrospective! *(See page 40)*
You can do this verbally and take notes, or on a large whiteboard, or a Kanban board

Hints and tips

- If you're using post-it notes, use three different colours to represent the headings. This means if they fall off the wall, you still know which section they belong to!
- Try to avoid prompting, let the feedback come from the participants.

 People over process

 Customer collaboration

 Responding to change

RETROSPECTIVES

Tell me about it

A Retrospective is an Agile ritual designed to take pause and reflect on how the team is going. The intent of the Retrospective is to identify what can be changed to improve performance. This is a terrific tool for change practitioners to use to educate the Agile team on importance of change management activities. It is a ritual of learning.

Sometimes Retrospectives are used as simply a way to keep good hygiene of the team, and sometimes they are deployed to fix problems. In this way, it gives the change practitioner a way to call out problems of not doing enough change management work.

There are many ways to run a Retrospective and the choice of which format depends on the focus of the improvement.

How do you use it?

Typically, you run them at the end of a designated period of time, such as a sprint, or a week, or a quarter.

Use a tool to capture the feedback. The more common ones are Kanban boards and flipcharts.

Ask the team to respond to a series of questions openly in front of each other.

Good to know

The quality of your Retrospective depends on the psychological safety of the team. If people don't feel safe to voice concerns or disappointment, then it is not likely to be a useful ritual for you.

We've included the standard three-column Retrospective – what worked, what didn't, what will we do better next time – on the previous page with Kanban examples.

You may also want to use a popular format from software company, Atlassian, called the 4 Ls – what did you like, what was lacking, what did you learn, what do you long for going forward?

Hints and tips

- Allocate a set time, also known as time-boxing the activity.
- People are often more open writing things down and posting their contribution on a board, than speaking out loud.
- Add a gratitude practice to the retro to really get people in a good headspace.
- Google 'retrospectives' to see a range of options to try – look for a blog post by Andy Cleff (details in the reference).

 People over process

 Customer collaboration

 Responding to change

FUTURE CHANGESCAPE

Tell me about it

Agile coach, Ben Linders, takes the Retrospective and flips it about to use it as a way of identifying what success looks like – this is your Future Changescape and it also identifies: what are the likely enablers and what are the potential obstacles that got in the way.

What we love about running this 'futurespective' is that the future-pacing of the activity de-personalises it and takes people out of a blaming mindset.

It becomes easy to deal with obstacles – mainly because they haven't happened yet!

How do you use it?

Tell your team they are 6, 12 or 18 months in the future.

They have been wildly successful and the change to be introduced has made a huge difference to the work life of many.

Ask them to spend some time describing that success with these questions in mind:

What were the practices, behaviours, skills and resources that got us here?

What were some of the obstacles that got in our way?

And how did we overcome them?

Good to know

There are multiple uses of Future Changescapes. You can use them with your project team to identify behaviours that will get in the way of a successful change implementation.

You can also use it at the beginning of a design phase to understand the enablers of successful change.

Hints and tips

- It can help to shift to a future state by asking them to close their eyes and do a short-guided meditation of what the future looks like.
- Be alert to language being used in the current state and remind them that they are describing things as if they are already in the future, rather than get caught up in talking about the past.

 People over process

 Customer collaboration

 Responding to change

CHANGE SCORECARD

Tell me about it

This is a way of taking the critical elements of change success (or your typical change readiness criteria) and displaying it using red, amber, green traffic lights to show progress in your change program. You put ownership of change readiness into the hands of the business stakeholder so they can have conversations with the Product Owner.

So, for example, some readiness criteria are:
- Leadership support
- Engaged change agents
- Audience is aware
- Audience understands why and what their role is in the change
- Audience is skilled and capable
- Audience is willing to change

How do you use it?

1. Determine what criteria that would indicate you're being successful.
2. Work out the groups you need to assess this against.
3. Pull this together on an A3 page or publish on your virtual platform.
4. Make a subjective assessment on where the groups are across the different criteria.
5. Put this poster up so it is visible.

Good to know

Don't be afraid of making your stakeholder groups amber or red.

You will be asked 'but why are these red?'

And that's your opportunity to have meaningful conversations with product owners, sponsors and leaders in the organization as to why it is so.

It catches their attention.

Hints and tips
- Create your change scorecard using PowerPoint so it's visual.
- Do not worry about accuracy – it's a conversation tool.

 People over process

 Customer collaboration

 Responding to change

APPLYING IT

ONGOING CHANGE SCORECARD

	DROP 1	DROP 2	DROP 3	DROP 4	CUSTOMERS
LEADERSHIP SUPPORT	○	○	●	●	●
CHANGE AGENTS ENGAGEMENT	●	●	●	●	●
AWARE	◔	◔	●	●	●
CAPABLE	●	●	●	●	●
WILLING	●	●	●	●	●
GENERATING IDEAS	◔	◔	●	●	●
LEARNING FEEDBACK LOOP ACTIVE	●	○	●	●	●

PERSONAS

Tell me about it

The use of Personas is another adaptation from design thinking and user experience toolkits.

Personas help us gain deeper insights into our employees and end-users so we can create a more user-friendly solution or future state.

It is a composite character profile that is fictional yet draws on several real characteristics rather than one typical customer or user.

How do you use it?

The more we know about our affected change recipients and end-users, the more likely we are to improve the overall experience with introducing the new product or service. In our world, that translates to higher adoption and more chance of landing the change successfully.

Good to know

A great way to introduce Personas to your project team and show the importance of change management on the initiative is to create them together in a workshop with the change recipients.

When you create the Persona with representatives from that user group, you are inviting early collaboration and deep engagement. Your change audience and end-users will strongly identify with a Persona they helped to create in a workshop.

To gain further insights into the creation of Personas, you can immerse yourself in their world by watching them, shadowing them and interviewing them.

Once you have your Persona, you have a great deal of data to use as input for your change artefacts.

Hints and tips

- You stop a Persona becoming a stereotype by using your data. Your data on the stakeholder grouping creates the composite character.
- Assign your Persona a fictional name and photograph or avatar.
- Build them with the people representing that Persona.

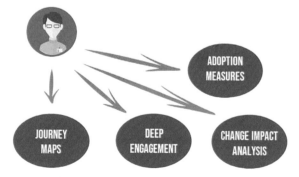

 People over process

 Customer collaboration

APPLYING IT

Building the Persona

Some Personas feature photographs, some feature avatars. Here's the typical features that appear in a Persona.

EMPLOYEE PERSONA

NEIL

BACKGROUND

- HR Business Partner
- Works in the Central Business District (CBD)
- Married with two children

DEMOGRAPHICS

- Middle management
- 38 years old
- University education
- Lives in South Eastern suburbs

IDENTIFIERS

- Uses organisation's platforms and systems everyday
- Ensures his team is on track to deliver their targets
- Finds it difficult to work collaboratively when people are using different systems
- Experiences challenges with limited options for customised reporting
- Spends a great deal of time managing and allocating resources

GUIDING STATEMENT

I want one HR system that we all use that customises reporting and tracks team members' activities and progress.

NOTES:

Part Five

ENGAGEMENT

IDEAS:

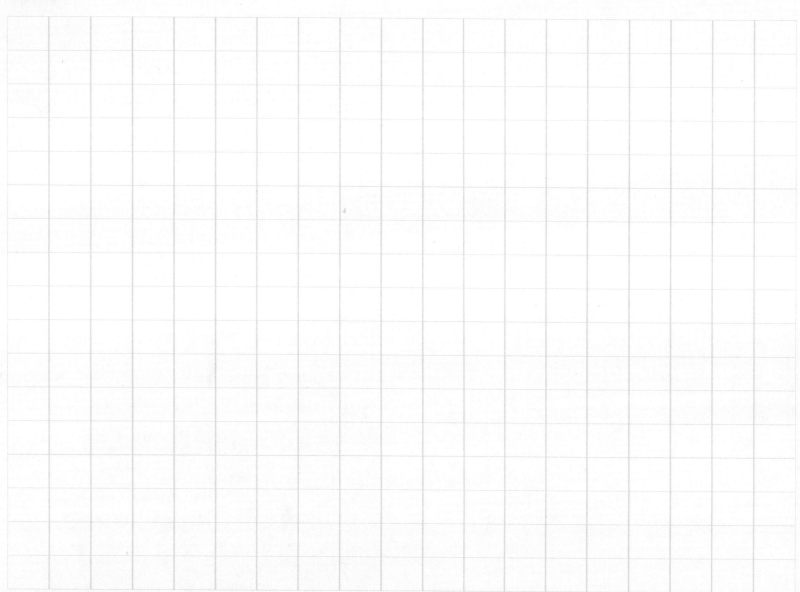

ENGAGEMENT

Engagement is incredibly important in agile change – it's how we ensure the integrity of the change.

To do this, we ask three questions:

> The amount of change resistance you experience is in inverse proportion to the amount of engagement you do.
> *Dr Jen Frahm*

WHO DO WE ENGAGE?

Social Architecture
The 3% rule

HOW DO WE GET BUY IN?

Co-creation including
60% Done and Shared
Lean Coffee
Reverse Go-Live
Change Ready Check

WHAT TOOLS DO WE USE?

Transparent Work Platforms such as:
Digital Kanban and workflow tools such as Jira
Enterprise Social Networks (ESNs) for social collaboration
Co-authoring tools such wikis
Change Canvas

A shift in focus

Whereas once our engagement activity was often more about - 'how do we socialise this idea?' - in agile change engagement, it's different. It's a genuine invitation to co-build and collaboratively develop the end product or service. If you are using your engagement activities solely to smooth adoption and sign-off, you are missing the point.

 People over process

 Working software

 Customer collaboration

 Responding to change

Look out for these icons to see which ones apply to each agile practice!

SOCIAL ARCHITECTURE

Tell me about it

Social Architecture is a concept pioneered in the change space by Belgian change practitioner, Luc Galoppin and plays to the need to find what are traditionally known as change champions, but also sustain the change post launch / release or go-live.

Traditionally, we looked to organizational charts that mapped the hierarchy for us to work out who we needed to engage with.

When we consider the Social Architecture of an organization, we recognise that organizational change is an activity that occurs within communities and networks.

Galoppin urges us to look to the white space that is between the boxes and lines of an organizational chart, to understand how to make change happen. As change practitioners, we need to design a Social Architecture to sustain our changes.

How do you use it?

- Identify communities that make change happen in your organization.
- Create opportunities for connection, identity and belonging.
- Think about who will live with your change after you leave the project.

Good to know

When we focus on the Social Architecture of the organization, we do not ignore the hierarchy.

A Social Architecture is a balancing act that ensures that the balance of control and compliance works with trust and co-creation.

Organizational Network Analysis is sometimes available from your ESN administrator.

There are also platforms like Swoop Analytics that are great for identifying online influencers within your organization.

Don't forget the old-fashioned way – who is it that people stop to chat to in the building?

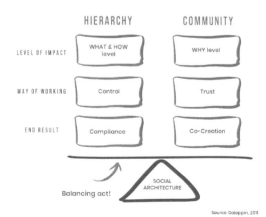

Source: Galoppin, 2011

Hints and tips

- Your ability to identify communities and community leaders is greatly enhanced by spending time on your Enterprise Social Network (ESN), e.g. Yammer, Workplace.
- Think about how your organizational change aligns with the purpose of the different communities.
- Don't try to control an influencer – they hate it. They need to be independent, not a spokesperson.
- Do ensure that you show appropriate gratitude for their efforts.
- Create forums with smaller groups to uncover the quieter achievers and influencers.

 People over process

APPLYING IT

Calling all Digital Pioneers

In one engagement, Dr Jen Frahm was leading an HRIS implementation. In starting this work, she found out it was part of a broader set of digital transformation activities. So, with the CIO's agreement, she established a new community on Yammer – called The Digital Pioneers.

Members were told that they were looking for pioneering spirits who were committed to collaboration, advocacy and inquiry of all things digital.

In joining this community, members would be expected to trial new technologies, provide feedback, act as buddies for colleagues struggling, and share resources about digital transformation.

The group had extraordinarily high uptake – many people wanted to belong to this exciting group. And once the HRIS was installed, members of this group turned their attention to the next change coming through.

The same organization also had an existing community of early career professionals. It was well established, with chapters in 28 geographies.

This was a well-established social tribe that could be accessed for sharing of information and recruiting of trainers for the technology changes.

THE 3% RULE

Another way to understand the Social Architecture is to apply Organizational Network Analysis (ONA). One vendor, Innovisor, carried out years of analysis to uncover some very interesting findings in relation to change. Their results showed that only 3% of your workforce are the KEY INFLUENCERS and they have the capacity to reach over 85% of your employees.

The trick is you need to find the right 3%!

If you do, they can build trust around your change initiative that makes it easier for your formal communication to be believed.

How do you use it?

- Start with estimating the number of people you need to be adopting your change to be successful? Is it 100, 1,000 or 5,000?
- Do the maths. For 100 people you need three influencers, for 1,000, you need 30, and for 5,000 people you need 150.
- Work out who is influential.
- Plan how you want to engage them.

People who are highly connected have twice as much power to influence change as people with hierarchical power.
Leandro Herrero

APPLYING IT

Leverage the research

Knowing about the 'three percent rule' prompts us to rethink how we deliver change.

When 3% of your workforce are the key influencers with the capacity to reach over 85% of your employees, the key is to find out who they are and how to leverage their impact.

When identifying stakeholders, it's not only the decision makers or people directly involved in the change who we need to consider.

Look beyond the formal organizational chart and hierarchy to uncover your hidden influencers. Informal power is often just as effective, if not more, than formal power when it comes to influence.

Carrying out an organizational network analysis will uncover these hidden influencers.

People listen to their peers because they trust them based on relationships already formed.

CO-CREATION

Tell me about it

The velocity and complexity of change today in our business means that we are not able to have access to all information required NOR able to control the direction. Collaborating through co-creation becomes an avenue to control a VUCA world.

Co-creation means we need to hand over the traditional control we had as specialists in our field to recognise that other people have specialised knowledge that is important and it is better to include them.

How do you use it?

- You can co-create change strategies, change plans, and communication platforms.
- You can also co-create the design of what the change is.

Good to know

Co-creation bolsters what is known as 'perceived control'.

When people perceive they have control in the outcome of a change, we know that the change is more likely to be successful.

Co-creation works better in situations with complex interdependencies.

Project managers often like you to show a plan or strategy to others and check they are okay with it.

This is not the same as co-creation.

Hints and tips

- Establish guiding principles that make it easy for people from diverse backgrounds to understand the outcomes.

```
VOLATILE
UNCERTAIN
COMPLEX
AMBIGUOUS

=VUCA
```

 People over process

 Customer collaboration

APPLYING IT

Run a Reverse Go-Live

A Reverse Go-Live is an excellent way to create a change plan collaboratively.

Start by finding a space (usually physical) that accommodates large sheets of paper to represent a time-line that is as long as your change project. You can also use an exceptionally long whiteboard.

At the far right of the paper, mark your go live date.

Assemble a diverse representative group of affected people in the space.

Give them post-it notes or index cards along with blu-tack or sticky putty.

Ask them to move to the far right of the wall where the Go-Live date is represented.

Note the date of the day before and write all the things that need to happen to be successful for Go-Live to happen on that day.

You then work backwards from the day before on the dependencies. For example, if we need the fact sheets printed, how long before they need to get to the printer, and then before that how long is the approval process, and how many rounds of this will need to happen.

When you work backwards, your brain is more likely to pick up the exceptions and show you the problems with timelines.

In fact, research shows people who plan backwards are more successful in achieving their goal.

When you involve others in the activity, it also highlights that some of the processes vary across division and geographies.

60% DONE AND SHARED

Once upon a time, in change management projects that used waterfall, it was not uncommon to have a very large word document that was your change strategy and plan.

On about page 4, it would list 20 reviewers and you would often be allowed about three months to develop this and complete it as a change deliverable (noted on a very big Gantt chart!). Your value as a change manager was dictated by the quality and perfection of the document. Once approved, there would be celebratory drinks and it would never be referred to again.

Agile Change throws this out the window!

Your task now is to create a change, communication and/or training strategy or plan to about 60% of the finished product and then share it with others as an act of co-creation.

As long as the strategy or plan can be understood, and it covers the best of what you know at the moment, it is good to be shared.

This is often a practice which will make a change manager feel quite vulnerable.

But ultimately, if your target audiences are co-creating your plan, they are unlikely to push back on it when you implement.

IDEAS:

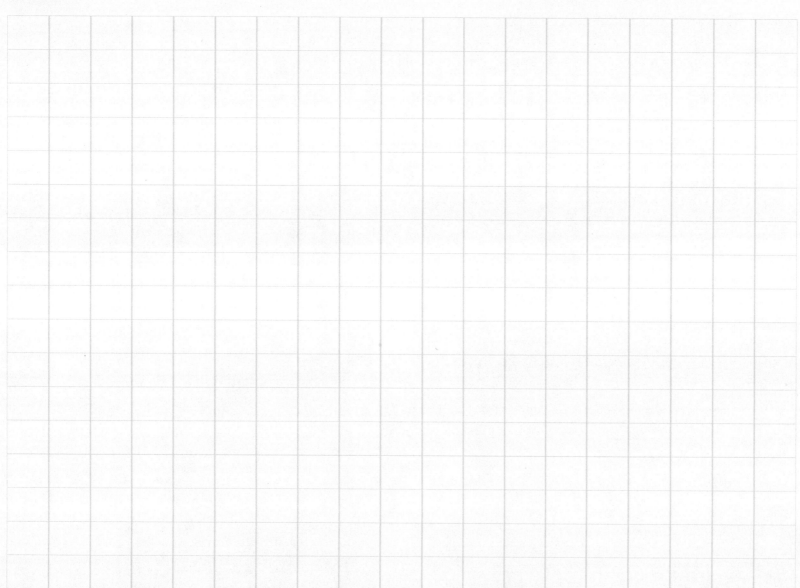

LEAN COFFEE

Tell me about it

'It was kind of an obvious development that Seattle - a city that is known for Starbucks headquarters and also a large technology scene - would be the homeland of 'Lean Coffee!'. This was the inspiration of Agile thought leaders Jim Benson and Jeremy Lightsmith.

Lean Coffee is a democratic meeting:
- With some structure and no agenda
- Where participants gather and decide on the agenda together
- That works best with 12 people or less.

We have a primal need for autonomy – so this forum gives every person a voice via a less formal engagement channel.

How do you use it?

You can use Lean Coffee for several purposes:
- Collaboratively develop the backlog of the changes to occur next
- Develop and respond to FAQS about the change
- Identify issues with implementation of change or enablers of organizational change
- Uncover early adopters and potential change champions
- Gather insights into topics and issues that are top of mind.

Good to know

This is not a forum for leaders to share information. All participants own the agenda.

This can also be run virtually using videoconferencing whiteboard facilities or shared screens or leancoffeetable.com

There is still a place for formal meetings in Agile, with agendas. Lean Coffees are designed to shift power to a broader audience.

> Agendas are so
> 20th century.
> *Jim Benson,*
> *Co-creator of Lean Coffee*

Hints and tips

- Limit people to one idea only. Tell them you will collect ALL ideas at the end so nothing is missed, and these can always be reviewed later.
- Take a photo of all the topics raised in case you need to revisit them.
- Time-box each discussion topic.
- Post photos of your session on your Enterprise Social Network (ESN).

 People over process

 Customer collaboration

LEAN COFFEE

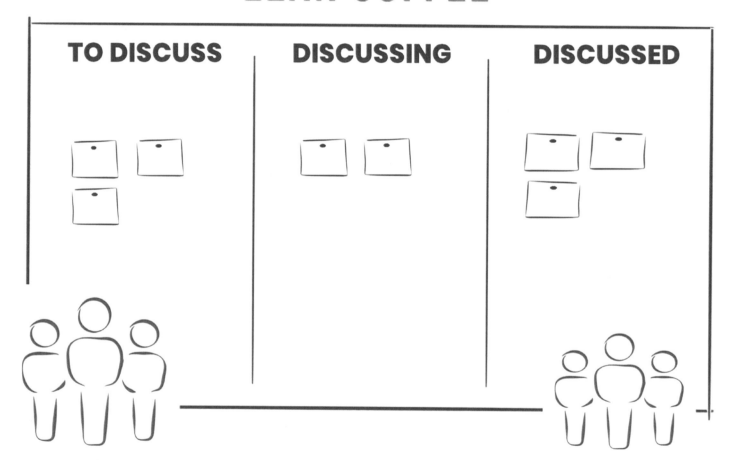

TO DISCUSS   DISCUSSING   DISCUSSED

LEAN COFFEE
HOW TO RUN ONE

1 Schedule your Lean Coffee session. Broadcast it widely including on your Enterprise Social Network (ESN) and Visual Management board.

2 Pack plenty of post-it notes, sharpie pens or markers and have a wall, whiteboard or virtual tool ready for the session with these three headings.

TO DISUSS | DISCUSSING | DISCUSSED

3 Kick off by explaining how the session will run.

4 Ask participants to write one topic they want to discuss on a post-it note and place it in the **TO DISCUSS** column.

5 Each participant introduces their topic in one or two sentences.

6 Each participant gets three votes. With either a small round sticker, or marking with a tick, they vote on the topic they want discuss.

7 They can assign votes in any way, e.g. three votes on one topic, one vote to three separate topics, or two to one topic and one to another. Votes determine the order of what's discussed.

8 Time-box each topic by agreeing on how long you want to spend on each one. When the time is up, vote with thumbs up or thumbs down to see if the group wants to continue with the topic or start the next one.

CHANGE READY CHECK

Tell me about it

A Change Ready Check is an agile version of a traditional change readiness assessment. Where this differs is you put the ownership of what it contains and how it is assessed in the hands of the business stakeholders.

You also use visual management principles to represent this in a large poster version.

It follows the traditional change curve-gates, e.g. Awareness, understanding and buy-in. In doing so, it adds gates that are relevant for the business stakeholder to be ready.

How do you use it?

It is particularly useful in environments where the business group needs to get ready for multiple releases.
You ask the team –'what is it that you need to be ready for this change?'
Typically, this looks like:

- We need to be aware of the release.
- We need to understand why it is happening and what it impacts.
- We need to have support material.
- We need training materials.
- We need to have a feedback loop if something goes wrong.

Good to know

You can also flip the use of this to where there is one change but multiple teams. This is very useful for change saturation!

In this instance, the poster is a visual for the team delivering the release.

This way, they can see at a glance the progress on which teams are ready for the release.

Hints and tips

- Keep it simple.
- Make sure it is the team leader who is responsible for ticking off the readiness element.
- This can be translated to Jira or other transparent workflow tools for an online version.

 People over process

 Customer collaboration

APPLYING IT

CHANGE READY CHECK

ONE CHANGE, MULTIPLE TEAMS

NAME OF CHANGE	New Dashboard Reporting		ACCOUNTABLE FOR ENSURING	Business Owner		
GROUP/TEAM	AWARE	UNDERSTAND WHY	TRAINING DELIVERED	USER SUPPORT CLEAR	CONFIDENT TO USE	ESCALATION PATH FOR ISSUES
TEAM 1						
TEAM 2						
TEAM 3						
TEAM 4						
TEAM 5						
TEAM 6						
TEAM 7						
TEAM 8						
TEAM 9						

CHANGE READY CHECK

ONE TEAM, MULTIPLE RELEASES

NAME OF TEAM	Call Centre Operations		ACCOUNTABLE FOR ENSURING	Business Owner		
GROUP/TEAM	AWARE	UNDERSTAND WHY	TRAINING DELIVERED	USER SUPPORT CLEAR	CONFIDENT TO USE	ESCALATION PATH FOR ISSUES
RELEASE 1						
RELEASE 2						
RELEASE 3						
RELEASE 4						
RELEASE 5						
RELEASE 6						
RELEASE 7						
RELEASE 8						
RELEASE 9						

TRANSPARENT WORK PLATFORMS

Tell me about it

Working on agile change is all about the speed of information to provide you feedback on effectiveness.

This speed of feedback is greatly enhanced when you use Transparent Work Platforms which permit real-time feedback.

Atlassian tends to dominate the agile domain with their products such as Confluence and Jira, but it is possible that you will be using other software platforms like Enterprise Social Networks (ESNs) such as Yammer or Workplace, or other digital Kanban tools like Trello or Asana.

How do you use it?

- Use ESNs to start conversations about the change you are implementing and to gather real-time feedback on how it is going.
- Leverage workflow tools as live issue-management across multiple geographies.

Good to know

There are three main purposes of Transparent Work Platforms:

1. Co-authoring
   E.g. wikis and collaborative documents
2. Project Management workflow
   E.g. digital Kanban tools like Trello, Jira, and Asana
3. Social collaboration
   E.g. Yammer, Workplace, Jabber

Hints and tips

- Check with your information security team on what you can post and what is not permitted.
- If you introduce tools that do not appear to be used elsewhere in your organization, check with your IT team for compatibility with other systems and if any help desk support is available.
- If you use a tool that has a smart phone application, life gets much easier - corridor conversations can be logged easily.

Customer collaboration

APPLYING IT

Co-authoring with collaborative document software

You can use wikis very effectively for real-time FAQs.

Set up the frame for the document and then provide access to employees to write their own questions.

In doing this, you then find that other members of the community will jump in and respond to the queries.

Ensure you have a subject matter expert available to verify crowd sourced responses.

Project management Digital workflow (e.g. Trello, Miro, Asana, Jira)

In one large technology implementation that Dr Jen Frahm was working on, they set up a Trello Board to represent all of the new functions that were being released.

Access was granted to every HR Business Partner across the globe and this became the place they could leave feedback and queries on adoption issues.

Note: This did not replace the technology bug register; it was solely focused on employee use and behaviour.

This meant that the change team had real-time visibility of adoption concerns and could prioritise and respond to these quickly.

Social collaboration with Enterprise Social Networks

Once you have used an ESN, such as *Yammer*, as a change tool, you are likely to find it challenging to work in environments where tools like this are absent.

ESNs are especially useful for:

- Facilitating connection and understanding
- Creating a public space for idea creation
- Identifying champions and purpose driven communities
- Non-hierarchical engagement
- Open and transparent communication

CHANGE CANVAS

Tell me about it

A Change Canvas is an excellent tool to engage sponsors and project directors to provide their perspective on what change needs to occur.

They are primarily vehicles to guide a conversation.

It's an adaptation of the 2004 Nine Box Business Model Canvas proposed by Swiss business theorist Alexander Osterwalder.

You can find many versions of the Change Canvas at leanchange.org

How do you use it?

- Work out what are the most useful talking points you need to engage stakeholders on. Typically, these will map to a change strategy outline -- so what is the change, who is affected, what are the impacts, why are we doing it.
- You can use this as a guide for one-on-one conversations or blow it up into a large size and have a group of people complete the sections with post-it notes.

Good to know

There is not a right or wrong way to present a Change Canvas. It is a visual tool for structuring a conversation and getting clear about what needs to happen.

Strategyzer has a range of canvases available through a creative commons license that you can adapt.

Hints and tips

- The template is a guide only – adjust it to suit your change initiative.
- Make it visible to all - post a colour copy in A3, or larger, on your Visual Management board.
- Carry a copy of your Change Canvas with you so you can refer to it in your conversations.

Customer collaboration

APPLYING IT

CHANGE CANVAS

PRODUCT OWNER		CHANGE LEAD	
CHANGE BEING INTRODUCED	What is the change?	Date	

PROBLEM (THE WHAT)	SOLUTION (THE HOW)	VALUE PROPOSITION (THE WHY)
		Why are we doing it?

CUSTOMERS/STAKEHOLDERS (WHO)	TIME & EFFORT NEEDED/CHANGE RESOURCES
Who is affected?	

COMMUNICATION		KEY IMPACTS	
EXISTING CHANNELS	KEY MESSAGES – W I I F M	EXISTING WAY OF WORKING	NEW WAY OF WORKING
			What are the impacts?

NOTES:

Part Six

COMMUNICATION

IDEAS:

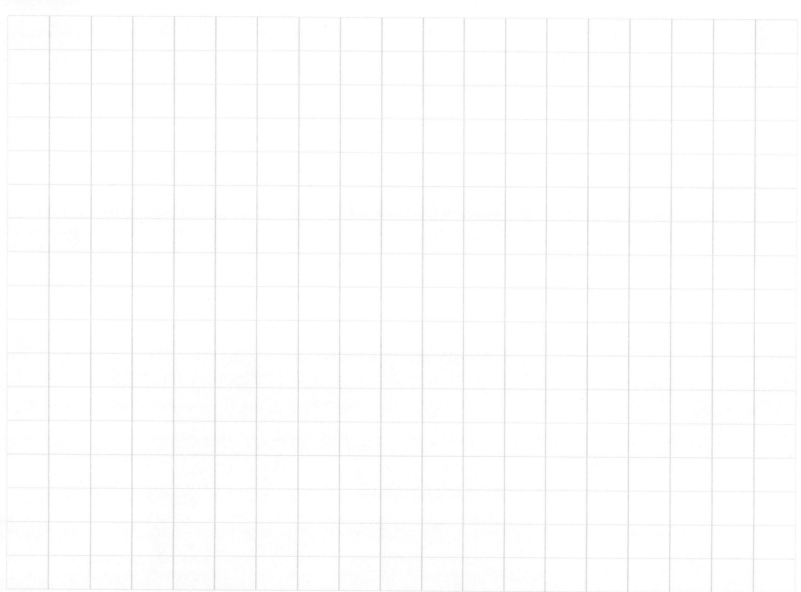

COMMUNICATION

There are three questions that inform our choice of communication practices on change initiatives:

> It seems that perfection is attained not when there is nothing more to add, but when there is nothing more to remove.
> *Antoine de Saint Exupéry*

HOW DO WE EFFICIENTLY KEEP UP WITH THE SPEED OF INFORMATION FLOW?
Stand-Ups
Plan-to-a-Page

HOW DO WE CREATE ENGAGING CHANGE COMMUNICATION?
Storytelling
Pecha Kucha
Lean Filmmaking

HOW DO WE GET PEOPLE'S ATTENTION WITH SO MUCH GOING ON?
Roadmaps
Infographics

A shift in focus
With the rapid iterations in agile initiatives, the change communication objective in agile projects shifts from 'how do I share information?' to 'how do I create communicative opportunities to generate more change?'

The biggest challenge for communications professionals in agile environments is the willingness to relinquish 'control of the message'.

Look out for these icons to see which ones apply to each agile practice!

 People over process

 Working software

 Customer collaboration

 Responding to change

STAND-UPS

Tell me about it

Stand-ups are short team progress meetings that are held frequently and are often the space where the change team can listen for change issues.

In organizations running 'scrum', they are known as daily scrum.

The benefits of Stand-ups are that they promote transparency.

Team members can raise awareness of blockers in real time.

How do you use it?

The key to a successful Stand-up is to make it short and limit the numbers in it to 5 to 10 people.

Stand-ups with 20 people soon become an extended meeting and few people enjoy standing for longer than 15 minutes.

The physical act of standing does promote brevity and focus.

Good to know

It's really important to be inclusive with Stand-ups, so this means thinking about how you include members of the team who are:
- Working remotely
- Geographically dispersed
- Across other time-zones
- Living with disability
- Have physical constraints.

Hints and tips
- Let your team know why you are running Stand-ups and what can be raised at a stand-up meeting.
- Create guiding principles for your stand-up.
- Assign someone to be a time-keeper.

People over process

APPLYING IT

THE TEAM STAND-UP
THE TYPICAL WAY TO GO

15
minutes
each
morning

What I did yesterday

What I'm doing today

What's getting in my way

PLAN-TO-A-PAGE

Tell me about it

The practice of creating a Plan-to-a-Page emerged with the recognition that many of the organization's leaders are too busy to read long documents.

So, to deliver change quickly, we need to be able to engage a stakeholder with what we plan to do and ensure they can see the role they will play in the change.

This has created the necessity to be good at rolling up 1,000-line project plans to create visually attractive 'one-pages' in PowerPoint.

How do you use it?

Carry the one page with you so you can easily pull it out to facilitate conversations with stakeholders about what will happen next.

Good to know

In agile projects, it is unlikely there is certainty about what is happening next beyond the next couple of sprints.

Your Plan-to-a-Page should reflect a time frame of no more than the next 12 weeks.

If your stakeholder wants a longer-term view then that is a Roadmap. *(See page 84)*

Hints and tips

- Your word count is at a premium, so be thoughtful about the headings you use and what they mean.
- Icons can be very useful in communicating details to save space.
- Check out icon libraries such as The Noun Project and Flat Icon. Even Office 365 has inbuilt iconography now!
- Don't forget version control!

🚶🚶 People over process

APPLYING IT

COMMUNICATIONS PLAN

CHANNELS	JUL-H1	JUL-H2	AUG-H1	AUG-H2	SEP-H1	SEP-H2
FACE TO FACE	Lean Coffee	Town Hall	Lean Coffee	Showcase	Town Hall	Lean Coffee
PROJECT POSTCARD	✉	✉	✉	✉	✉	✉
INTRANET	Set up site					
ENTERPRISE SOCIAL NETWORK		Kick off group	Yam Jam		Yam Jam	
VISUAL MANAGEMENT	Set up wall	Introduce personas	Kanban			
EXISTING FORUMS	Steering Committee ◆			◆		◆
	GM Check In Meeting ◇			◇		◇

STORYTELLING

Tell me about it
Social scientist and researcher, Dr Brene Brown, tells us that stories are 'data with a soul'.

This is a more engaging way of sharing the change strategy or a change vision.

Stories create intimacy in connecting with your people as they are often more personal and relevant than communicating through points on PowerPoint slides.

People are essentially social beasts and our knowledge is often transmitted and shared through story.

How do you use it?
Stories are effective when people are overwhelmed with facts and figures. Stories are sticky, so leverage their viral nature.

You can use stories to:
- Launch an idea
- Build trust
- Relate to people – they empathise with the storyteller
- Explain the 'why'.

Good to know
There is immense power in 'story gathering'. Your people will have many stories to share of how your change can benefit them.

Stories need to be embedded in authenticity. If people don't believe the story, it can be damaging to your initiative.

Pixar also has a famous and proven process for building stories. Check out their template on how to use this on *page 78*.

Hints and tips
- Situate in time – a story has a time marker.
- Situate in place – a story has a place marker.
- Include a set of events - linked things that happen.
- Introduce characters – includes dialogue and makes it real.
- Weave in something unanticipated.

Source: Shawn Callahan, Anecdote

Must read: Putting Stories to Work by Shawn Callahan

 People over process

APPLYING IT

Dr Jen Frahm once worked with a leader with a masterful story. The change initiative was to build a digital project management portal. The Program Director would start each meeting with new stakeholders with a simple story.

'Do you remember the time when you got your first iPhone? I do. I was so excited. I opened the beautiful white box and took the phone out. And I lifted up the packaging. Carefully, sifted through. And I was outraged. Apple had forgotten to put the instructions in! I was so annoyed – I really didn't want to go back into the Apple store.

And then I just pushed the button at the bottom of the phone. And it was quite magical. The phone came on. And it walked me through the set up. In plain English. It was so easy! I didn't need instructions. Five minutes later I was off and running and using my new phone.

That's the experience I want our people to have with this portal. Just push the button. Easy. Intuitive. No training necessary.

Three months later, Jen had a meeting with one of the country managers – and he pulled out his iPhone and said to her...'Do you remember the time when you got your first iPhone?'

The managers had fully embraced the vision of the change and now owned it, thanks to a very simple little story.

THE PIXAR FORMULA
TO STRUCTURE YOUR STORY

ONCE THERE WAS	EVERY DAY	THEN ONE DAY	BECAUSE OF THAT	UNTIL FINALLY
The current state, often the state that needs to change	What's going on in this state?	Something happened!	So what are we doing about it now?	What does the future look like?
	What's **not** going on in this state that should be?	Describe any conflict, challenge, issues, pain points or problems	And because of that	Define the solution to the problem
		Make it personal – provide names & describe emotions	And this is how we are doing it	Don't forget to mention the benefits!

SOURCE: Based on Pixar's rules of storytelling, originally by Emma Coats

IDEAS:

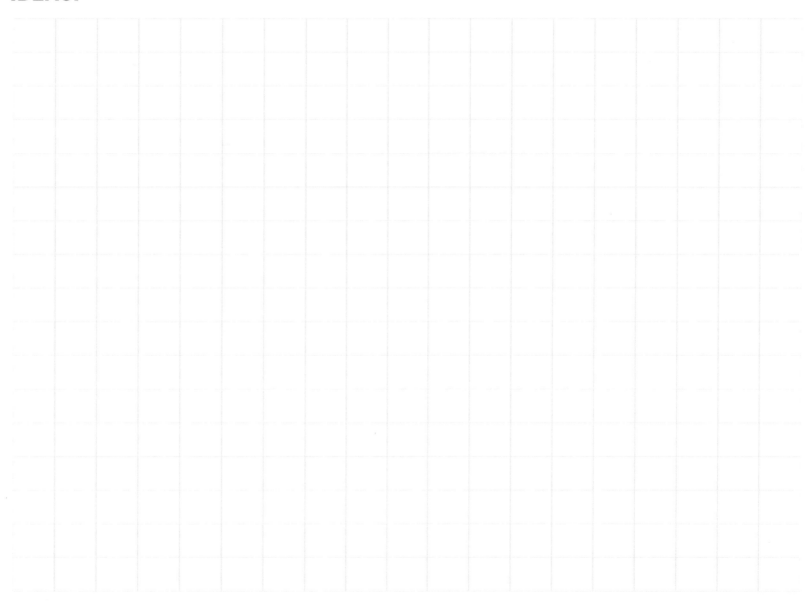

PECHA KUCHA

Tell me about it

Pecha Kucha is a Japanese word for 'chit-chat'. It became popular in Tokyo in 2003 when started by a couple of architects.

It is a form of visual storytelling where you use 20 slides in 20 minutes to tell a story.

We have seen it adapted in many forms – sometimes six slides in six minutes, often referred to as a 'lightning talk'.

The focus on images over words, along with the fast pace, keeps you focused on what you want to say.

The bite-size nature of the communication makes it very brain-friendly.

How do you use it?

You can use it for several purposes.

For example, it's an engaging way to share a new strategy or change objective.

It can also be a form of 'Working Out Loud' or agile showcasing so you can use it to share work in progress and invite people to contribute. In this way, it changes the frame from providing information to co-creating change through a communicative process.

Good to know

Presenting in six, 10 or even 20 minutes is really hard!

You need to get good at what you do NOT say.

It's okay to stumble as you go, your audience appreciates the pressure of the task and can relate to the difficulty you face.

Hints and tips

- Head to royalty-free sites such as unsplash.com or pixabay.com to source great images.

Keep it visual:

- Slides with facts and figures do not work.

Record your sessions so they can be:

- Shared across locations
- Accessed by people who missed out
- Watched again

People over process

APPLYING IT

PECHA KUCHA
HAVE A GO!

You're presenting to a new team and you only have six minutes.

Story board
1. What you want to share.
2. What is the most important thing for them to know.

GO!

6 SLIDES IN 6 MINUTES

LEAN FILMMAKING

Tell me about it

Lean Filmmaking is a relatively new discipline developed by siblings Kylie Eddy (a filmmaker) and David Eddy (an agile coach) - to overcome the long and high-risk process of traditional filmmaking.

It's based on four core principles:

- Collaboration is compulsory.
- Story before production values.
- Be fan focused first.
- Choose doing over planning.

How do you use it?

We've used Lean Filmmaking several times on change projects for bite-sized change communication. Most phones now have a video application and there are many cost-effective editing apps.

You can use Lean Filmmaking to:
- Capture work in progress and showcase it via your Enterprise Social Network (ESN)
- Create mini films of user cases for the project team to understand the user needs
- Develop micro-learning snippets
- Share highlights from your engagement.

Good to know

In corporate life, 90 seconds is probably as long as you can go in holding people's attention.

TikTok is showing you can create really engaging videos in as short as 15 seconds.

When people's attention span is overwhelmed, you can cut through with short and snappy content.

Work with a pyramid structure of message composition – share the core message first and broaden out to less important details. This means if they have limited time, they get the key message quickly before they tune out with the details.

Hints and tips

- 2/3 of viewers will watch a clip to the end if less than 60 seconds.
- Map out a series of short videos to tell your story.
- Have your recipients of change craft the videos and star in them – it's a great engagement activity and it's better to hear the story in their words not the project's words.

New book coming soon – Lean Filmmaking by Kylie Eddy and David Eddy.

 Working software

APPLYING IT

Have a go!

While not technically Lean Filmmaking, this is a great activity to get you used to not overthinking and overproducing your video content. You choose doing over planning! And it's all about story over production values.

Think about something in a current project that you could share in a 60 second video.

- What is the story to tell?
- Who needs to be in it?
- How will you share it?

Your tools are:

- A smartphone
- 'Splice' editing app

LIGHTS

CAMERA

ACTION!

ROADMAPS

Tell me about it

On agile initiatives we often have more certainty about what is happening in the next two weeks and less certainty with what happens further down the track.

This means that creating detailed change and communication plans is difficult to do and often a waste of time and effort.

For this reason, it can be helpful to move to using Roadmaps which are a visual depiction of the road ahead. Because of the high-level information, it is easy to update and change as new information comes to light.

Ultimately the Roadmap communicates the strategy, not the plan.

How do you use it?

Create your Roadmaps using PowerPoint and then print them in A3 size.

Carry them with you for stakeholder meetings so you have them handy to show the stakeholder where you are at the moment and what comes next.

You can use Roadmaps for:
- Technology rollouts
- Product delivery
- Change activity
- Communication calendar
- Training and development.

Good to know

Roadmaps don't need to be highly accurate.

They do need to have some time marking – this can be weeks, months, quarters or years.

Roadmaps provide crucial context for teams.

They answer the question:
Where do I belong in this journey?

Hints and tips
- If you use collaborative project management tools to do your road mapping any changes made are automatically available to all stakeholders who have access.
- Never roadmap alone – this is an essential act of co-creation and engagement.

People over process

APPLYING IT

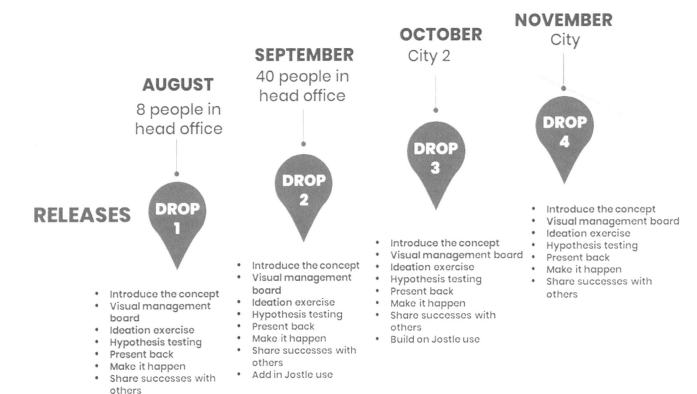

AGILITY ROADMAP

RELEASES

AUGUST
8 people in head office

DROP 1
- Introduce the concept
- Visual management board
- Ideation exercise
- Hypothesis testing
- Present back
- Make it happen
- Share successes with others

SEPTEMBER
40 people in head office

DROP 2
- Introduce the concept
- Visual management board
- Ideation exercise
- Hypothesis testing
- Present back
- Make it happen
- Share successes with others
- Add in Jostle use

OCTOBER
City 2

DROP 3
- Introduce the concept
- Visual management board
- Ideation exercise
- Hypothesis testing
- Present back
- Make it happen
- Share successes with others
- Build on Jostle use

NOVEMBER
City

DROP 4
- Introduce the concept
- Visual management board
- Ideation exercise
- Hypothesis testing
- Present back
- Make it happen
- Share successes with others

THE VISION
Build-measure-cycles ● Progressively amplify based on learning ● Work Out Loud

INFOGRAPHICS

Tell me about it

An Infographic is a visual representation of data in a way that is easy to digest. It relies heavily on icons and pictures with minimal text.

It's a brain-friendly method of communication as it makes it easy to associate images with messages.

Once you needed a graphic designer to do this, but now advances in PowerPoint and easy-to-use software means anyone can bring their change communication to life with engaging communication.

How do you use it?

You can use infographics to:
- Provide quick overviews of a topic
- Show change impacts at a glance
- Simplify complex processes
- Share research findings that justify your change
- Compare and contrast current state and future state.

Good to know

There are three main uses of infographics:
- Data visualisation
- Information design
- Change narrative display.

The majority of infographics in change programs are static, but if you have the budget you may wish to develop interactive infographics.

Hints and tips

- Canva has numerous templates for infographics.
- Piktochart is easy to use.
- You can create infographics in PowerPoint.
- Source an icon library, e.g. Noun Project.
- If you are entering company information into an infographic software platform, make sure you check with Infosec on whether it is safe to do so, as some platforms have loose information security and are associated with public breaches.
- Ask your marketing and communications team if they have a corporate account with any subscription, or if they have their own library, so you can access brand colours and assets.

 People over process

APPLYING IT

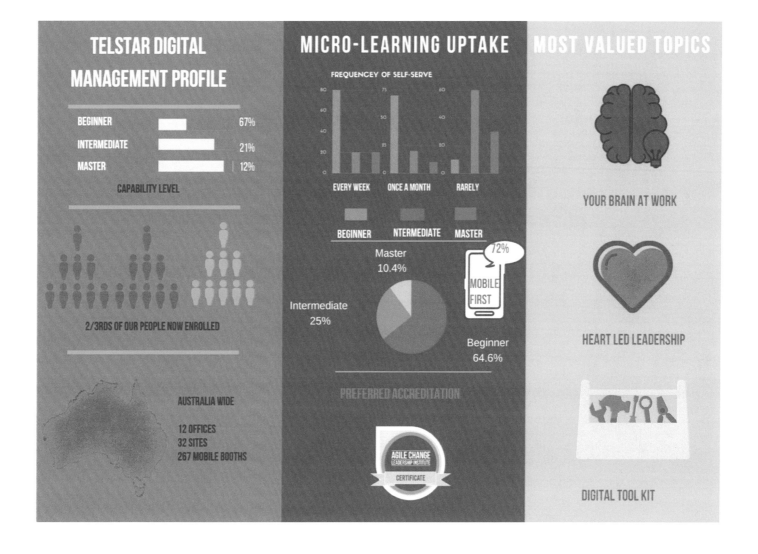

NOTES:

Part Seven

SO WHAT, NOW WHAT?

PARTING WORDS

Each organization has different characteristics in nuances, culture and industry type; and each will be best served by a change approach that is right for them in size and nature at that point in time.

The art of agile change management is to recognise the unique characteristics of both the organization and the project, and to devise a plan that stays true to your agreed principles yet is adaptive in its development and delivery.

This means that the role of the change practitioner is an emerging and changing role, and it demands a nimble approach to meet the ongoing challenges faced by organizations.

Whilst the future of change management as a practice looks optimistic, we also need to play a role in nurturing our own professional development to transform business challenges into opportunities.

We're really looking forward to building this Playbook to be even bigger. Do make sure you let us know of any major successes you have trying these, and yes, do tell us when they don't work – this is how we learn.

If you want access to a short presentation on how to adapt your traditional change management framework with these 30 Agile Change tools by using our 'Map, Identify and Simplify' approach please let us know, we'll send you a link!

But in parting, why not use the next few pages to assess your own capabilities and confidence in using the agile change practices we have shared and have some fun exploring.

In the words of Walt Disney...

I can never stand still. I must explore and experiment. I am never satisfied with my work. I resent the limitations of my own imagination.

A PERSONAL STOCKTAKE - HOW DO YOU RATE?

 People over process   Customer collaboration

 Data informed Decision Making   Engagement   Communication

 Working software   Responding to change

PRACTICE	Agile value	Capability	Never tried it	Won't work here	Keen to try	Some experience	All over it!
Work Out Loud	🏃⚙️👥↻	●●●					
Change Data Use	↻	●●●					
Visual Management	🏃⚙️👥↻	●●●					
Kanban Board	🏃⚙️👥↻	●●●					
MVCP	⚙️👥	●					
Change Backlog	⚙️👥	●					
User Stories	⚙️👥	●					
T-Shirt Sizing	⚙️👥	●					
Story Points	⚙️👥	●					
Change Blast Radius	🏃👥	●					
Change Radar	🏃👥	●					

PRACTICE	Agile value	Capability	Never tried it	Won't work here	Keen to try	Some experience	All over it!
Think Act Feel	👥👥	●●					
I like, I wish, what if?	👥👥↻	●●					
Retrospective	👥👥↻	●●					
Future Changescape	👥👥↻	●					
Change Scorecard	👥👥↻	●●					
Persona	👥👥	●●					
Social Architecture	👥	●					
3% Rule	👥	●					
Co-Creation	👥👥	●					
Reverse Go-Live	👥	●					
60% Done and Shared	⚙👥	●●					
Lean Coffee	👥👥	●					
Change Ready Check	👥↻	●					
Transparent Work Platforms	👥	●●					
Collaborative Document Authoring	👥	●●					
Digital Workflow	👥	●●					

PRACTICE	Agile value	Capability	Never tried it	Won't work here	Keen to try	Some experience	All over it!
Enterprise Social Networks (ESNs)	👥	●●					
Change Canvas	⚙ 👥	●●					
Stand-Ups	👪	●					
Plan-to-a-Page	👪	●					
Storytelling	👪	●					
Pecha Kucha	👪 ⚙	●					
Lean Filmmaking	👪 ⚙	●					
Roadmaps	👪 ⚙	●					
Infographics	👪	●					

NOTES:

REFERENCES

THE AGILE MANIFESTO

The Agile Manifesto, values and principles on
https://agilemanifesto.org/
https://medium.com/@ameet/what-musk-bezos-thiel-and-feynman-teach-us-about-first-principles-261967d3e347

AGILE CHANGE TOOLS AND PRACTICES

https://thebryceswrite.com/2010/11/29/when-will-we-work-out-loud-soon/
Stepper, J. (2015), *Working Out Loud For a Better Career and Life,* John Stepper Self Published.
https://www.cultureamp.com/
https://www.swoopanalytics.com/
https://www.campaignmonitor.com/
https://mailchimp.com/
https://www.microsoft.com/en-au/microsoft-365/yammer/yammer-overview
https://www.facebook.com/workplace

DATA INFORMED DECISION MAKING

Stanford d.school Bootleg Camp - PDF toolkit resource available online on their website
https://dschool.stanford.edu/resources/design-thinking-playbook-from-design-tech-high-school
https://www.atlassian.com/team-playbook/plays/retrospective
https://www.benlinders.com/Ben is an agile coach who has written a lot about retrospectives and futurespectives. He has presentations on SlideShare too.
http://www.andycleff.com/category/retrospectives/

ENGAGEMENT

https://www.managementexchange.com/hack/social-architecture-manifesto
https://www.innovisor.com/2017/05/30/how-to-rethink-change-with-the-three-percent-rule/
http://leancoffee.org/
https://leancoffeetable.com/
https://trello.com/
https://asana.com/
https://www.atlassian.com/
https://www.cisco.com/c/en/us/products/unified-communications/jabber/index.html
https://leanchange.org/
https://www.strategyzer.com/canvas/business-model-canvas
Williams, Wil & Lewis, Duncan. (2008). Strategic management tools and public sector management. *Public Management Review*. 10.
  10.1080/14719030802264382.

COMMUNICATION

https://www.ted.com/talks/brene_brown_the_power_of_vulnerability
https://laughingsquid.com/22-rules-of-storytelling/
https://www.pechakucha.com/
https://leanfilmmaking.com/
https://splice.com/
https://www.canva.com/
https://piktochart.com/
https://pixabay.com/

RECOMMENDED READING

Callahan, S. (2016), *Putting Stories to Work*, Pepperberg Press, Melbourne

Dweck, C. S. (2006), *Mindset: The New Psychology of Success*, Ballantine Books, New York

Frahm, J. Dr. (2017), *Conversations of change: A Guide to Implementing Workplace Change*, Jennifer Frahm Collaborations, Melbourne.

Heimans, J. & Timms, H. (2018), *New Power: How Power Works in Our Hyperconnected World and How to Make It Work for You*, Macmillan, Sydney.

Johansen, B. (2009), *Leaders Make the Future: Ten New Leadership Skills for an Uncertain World,* Academy of Management Executive, Berrett-Koehler, San Francisco.

Landsberg, M. (1996), *The Tao of Coaching: Boost your effectiveness at work by inspiring and developing those around you,* Harper Collins, London

Lawrence, K. (2013), *Developing Leaders in a VUCA Environment*, UNC Kenan-Flagler Business School, White Paper.

Ries, E. (2011), *The Lean Startup*, Portfolio Penguin, St Ives

Ross, L. (2017), *Hacking for Agile Change: With an agile mindset, behaviours and practices*, Green Hill, Adelaide.

Ross, L. (2020), *Change Management The Essentials: The modern playbook for new and experienced practitioners,* Green Hill, Adelaide

Stanford Institute of Design, d.school, Bootleg Bootcamp

TED talk (2014) by Jeremy Heimans – *'What new power looks like'*

Weick, K. E. (1996), The story about the fire-fighters: Drop your tools: An allegory for organizational studies *Administrative Science Quarterly*, Vol. 41, pp. 301-313

https://www.jstor.org/stable/2393722?seq=1

ABOUT THE AUTHORS

DR JEN FRAHM

Jen is a tamer of ambiguity, speaker of truths and solver of problems. She is the founder of Conversations of Change, a podcaster, a blogger and a global expert on organizational change and transformation

She has delivered across multiple industries and professions, from wine sales to wedding dresses, veterinary products to energy retailers, nuns and engineers, big banks, small IT companies, publicly listed, privately owned and non-profit organizations.

A sought-after speaker, she is known for being at the frontier of agile change practice.

She has a PhD in Management and has taught in Australia's leading Universities.

Jen's first book, *Conversations of Change*: *A guide to implementing workplace change* was released in July 2017.

LENA ROSS

As an experienced change consultant, Lena established her consulting practice #changehacks in 2016 and has since made a significant contribution to the change management profession.

Her work has taken her across many locations including Silicon Valley, to run workshops and consult to senior leaders on building agile capability.

Lena's work draws on the latest thinking in change management from areas such as design thinking, future of work, digital, hardwired human behaviour and agile mindset and approaches.

Her experience is complemented by her Master of Business Administration (MBA) qualification, and she applies academic and business discipline to develop practical and innovative solutions.

Lena's first book *Hacking for Agile Change* was released in July 2017. Her second book *Change Management The Essentials* was released in February 2020.

Jen and Lena are both skilled educators and coaches with backgrounds in learning and development, and academia and are known for being at the frontier of change, agile and learning. They are straight shooters with an empathic approach.

After several successful collaborations they formed the Agile Change Leadership Institute in 2019.

CPSIA information can be obtained
at www.ICGtesting.com
Printed in the USA
LVRC091258140521
687291LV00003B/10